If God Is Your Co-Pilot, Switch Seats

Miracles Happen When You Let Go!

BJ Gallagher

HAMPTON ROADS

Copyright © 2011 by BJ Gallagher

Cover design by Jim Warner
Interior design by Kathryn Sky-Peck

Hampton Roads Publishing Company, Inc.
Charlottesville, VA 22906

www.hrpub.com

Library of Congress Cataloging-in-Publication Data
available upon request.

ISBN: 978-1-57174-648-1

GWP

10 9 8 7 6 5 4 3 2 1

Printed in Hong Kong

Dedication

To my spiritual friends;

"We teach best what we need to learn most," William James wrote. That's certainly true for me. I've spent six decades trying to learn how to live in right relationship with other people, right relationship with myself, and most importantly — right relationship with God. I've longed to live a surrendered, faith-full life — letting God run the Universe.

But it's not easy for a type-A girl like me — headstrong, impulsive, raised to be independent and self-reliant. No sooner do I get into alignment with Divine Order, than I find myself trying to take control again. It seems I'm a slow learner . . . as well as a *fast forgetter!*

This slender volume is a collection of words of wisdom about the gifts of spiritual surrender. I've gathered some very personal stories and poems here, along with pearls of inspiration, golden nuggets, and priceless gems from my favorite spiritual teachers (including some rather unlikely teachers) in order to share them with you.

In-joy! BJ

Contents

It is in our faults and failings, not in our virtues,
that we touch one another and find sympathy.
It is in our follies that we are one.

—Jerome K. Jerome, English writer

Introduction

Spiritual wisdom often shows up in the most unlikely places. The title of this book came from a bumper sticker I spotted while driving on an L.A. freeway. I wasn't looking for spiritual guidance at that moment — at least I didn't think I was. But when I read the bumper sticker, I knew the message was for me.

That's the thing about spiritual wisdom — it has an uncanny way of showing up at just the right moment, in just the right format. The medium may be unlikely, but that doesn't invalidate the message. The teacher sometimes seems questionable, but the validity of his or her teaching is unmistakable. Spiritual guidance resonates with the ring of truth, no matter what the guise of medium or messenger.

Wisdom can come out of the mouths of babes — or taxi drivers, bartenders, therapists, mothers, and others.

Wisdom can be found on bumper stickers or on the walls of public bathrooms. Wisdom can be disguised as an offhand comment or dressed up in a fancy sermon. Wisdom is scribbled on a cocktail napkin, a to-do list, or the back of an envelope. Wisdom sprouts here and there on websites and blogs. Wisdom sometimes cracks wise on late night TV, or reads somber and serious in a newspaper op-ed. Wisdom can glare from a neon sign, or whisper gently from a church marquee. Wisdom has been discovered carved on stone tablets, written in ancient scrolls, or bound between book covers.

It doesn't matter where you find wisdom — as long as you put it to good use.

It is my hope that you'll find wisdom that speaks to you in this volume. But make no mistake — I am the messenger, not the message. I've always liked how Mother Teresa described her work:

I am a little pencil in the hand of a writing God who is sending a love letter to the world.

I don't think she'd mind if I adopted and adapted my own version:

I am a laptop in the hands of God who is sending an e-book of love to the world.

Surrender

Surrender

Have you ever lost your car keys?

You look
      and look
           and look
                and look . . .

until finally,
      you run out of places to search.

So you go back and look
in all the old places
      again
           and again
                and again.
But, alas,
      no keys.

Finally . . .
      exhausted,
      frustrated,
      hopeless,
      and out of steam,
           you throw your hands in the air —
           "I give up!"

The keys are lost.
You let go
        and move on.

Just about then
        the most amazing thing happens . . .
Suddenly . . .
        sometimes immediately . . .
                your keys turn up.

"Ha!
There they are —
        right in front of me!"
                you exclaim.
"How about that!"

Your day is made —
        what was given up for lost
                is amazingly found.
And all is right with the world again.

"What a miracle!"
          you marvel.

And you're right —
          it's the miracle of surrender.

When you finally give up
trying to solve all your problems
by yourself . . .
          When you stop struggling
          and accept life on life's terms . . .
                    When you admit
                    that you can't control the world
          around you . . .
That's when miracles happen.

Let go and let God . . .
          Experience the miracle of surrender.

Surrender makes you
FAITH-FULL . . .

Surrender makes you . . .

Freedom from Fear

F
A
I
T
H
F
U
L
L

Faith

When you come to the edge
of all the light that you know
and are about to drop off into
the darkness of the unknown,
faith is knowing one of two things will happen:
There will be something solid to stand on,
or you will be taught to fly.

~ Patrick Overton, author, poet, educator

Just the Two of Us

I'll never forget that first night in our new apartment. I had spent the previous week getting the place ready for us to move into, as I prepared for the next chapter in my life — a single mom going back to college with my four-year-old son, Michael, in tow.

We had lived with my parents in Dover, Delaware, for a year after my marriage broke up — they were so patient and generous as they gave me space and time to figure out what I was going to do with the rest of my life. I was just 23 years old — disappointed in love and confused about my future. I finally decided I needed to go to college and get an education.

I had very little money to start my new life — just $100 a month child support and $100 a month from my parents. I rented a basement apartment in Newark, where the University of Delaware was located — a hundred miles north of Dover. I furnished it with a $10 army cot for Michael, a $40 used bed for myself, a $10 table on which to study, and two empty beer kegs with pillows on top for stools. My coffee table was two cinderblock bricks with a board across the top. There was no sofa, just a small Greek flokati rug to sit on the floor. A bookcase held my radio/receiver, turntable, and a pair of small stereo speakers. The place looked like a typical college student apartment — except that in our case, the student was a young single mother with a toddler.

Michael and I spent our first day unpacking and putting our clothes and personal things away in the closets and cabinets. His toys filled a plastic laundry basket. We went to the market to stock up on food and got the kitchen all ready to use. It had been a busy day.

Bedtime came and after his bath, I knelt to tuck Michael into his army cot. Tears welled up in his eyes as I leaned over to kiss him goodnight. "I'm scared," he started to cry. "I want to go back to Grandma's house."

I wrapped my arms around him. "I know, sweetheart. I want to go back to Grandma's house too," I said as I started to cry, too. "But we can't — we have to stay here and start our new life. From now on it's just you and me."

We clung to each other and sobbed. We felt like a couple of orphans, suddenly finding ourselves alone that night, knowing we had to make our own way in the world. We were both scared, not knowing what the future held for us.

As our tears subsided, we just hugged each other. I offered up a silent prayer, asking for help. When Michael finally fell asleep in my arms, I went off to sleep in my own room.

That was many years ago and, needless to say, we survived that night. There were many more challenges in the following days, weeks, months, and years — and many a time I turned to prayer.

Being a single parent was the hardest thing I've ever done. Countless times I felt clueless. Often, I asked Michael's father for advice; occasionally I asked friends who were parents, too. But most often I turned to God, seeking help with all the problems that parenthood brings.

I've often joked to friends that Michael and I took turns raising each other. But the real truth is — God had to raise both of us at the same time!

Faith is taking the first step even when

you don't see the whole staircase.

~ Rev. Martin Luther King Jr.,
civil rights leader

What Are You Waiting For?

A wise woman once wrote,
    "It's never too late
      to be what you might have been."

I want to believe her,
    but I'm afraid . . .

afraid I won't succeed,
afraid others will think me foolish,
afraid that I can't change,
afraid I don't have enough time,
    talent,
        energy,
            focus,
                or persistence.

Deep down,
    I worry that maybe it IS too late
      for me.

"What are you waiting for?"
    God asks.

"I'm waiting for the right time,"
        I reply.

"No time like the present,"
        God smiles.

"I'm waiting for more information,"
        I explain.

"You have all the information you need,"
        God persists.

"I'm waiting for the fear to subside,"
        I confess.

"I'm right here with you —
just feel your fear
and do it anyway,"
        God nudges.

• • • ➡

"How?"

      I plead.

"How do I do that?"

"The answer to 'how' is 'yes,'"

      God explains.

"Say 'yes' to taking the first step.

      Say 'yes' to getting into action.

            Say 'yes' to moving forward.

Say 'yes' to change.

      Say 'yes' to life.

            Just say 'yes.'"

just say yes . . .

Belief Versus Trust

Several years ago I heard a wonderful story about a man named George who wanted to ride his bicycle on a thick cable strung across Niagara Falls. He showed up at the falls one morning, and as he prepared for his ride, a crowd began to gather. Everyone was excited. "You can do it, George!" they cheered. "We believe in you!" As the crowd grew larger, you could feel their enthusiasm in the air.

George finally finished his preparations, mounted his bike and positioned it on the cable, then pedaled off across the falls. Everyone yelled encouraging words: "Keep going, George! You're doing great! We believe in you! You can do it!"

George balanced his bike skillfully and gracefully as he pedaled over the roaring falls below. Finally, he reached the other side and the crowd erupted in joy! They screamed and yelled in happiness. Then, much to their surprise and delight, George turned his bike around and pedaled back over the falls once again, to end up where he'd started.

As he completed his return trip, the gathered crowd was ecstatic. "George, you're amazing! Bravo! We knew you could do it! We had faith in you all along!" They cheered, laughed, and hugged George, clapped him on the back, and heaped their joyful praise upon him. It was a wonderful scene.

Then George surprised the crowd again. He said, "I'm going to do it again, but this time I'm going to take one of you with me. Who wants to ride on my handlebars?"

The crowd fell silent. People looked askance at one another. An eyebrow here and there was raised. Folks hung back. It looked like no one would ride with George.

But then a little girl who'd been watching from the sidelines stepped forward. "I'll go with you," she said.

George smiled and scooped the little girl up in his arms. As he carried her toward his bike, the crowd grew angry. "You can't take that little girl," they yelled. "It's too dangerous!" They looked around for someone to stop him. "Somebody call the authorities — he should be arrested! Don't let him take that little girl!"

But George paid no attention to their protests. He put the girl on his handlebars, showed her where to hold on, and then pedaled off across the falls again.

The crowd was furious — and terrified. They screamed for him to come back. Some cried. Others looked away, afraid to witness the tragedy they anticipated. A few fell silent and held their collective breath.

George kept pedaling, maintaining his focus and concentration. The little girl held tight, just as she'd been shown. And soon, the two reached the other side.

Without so much as a second thought, George turned the bike around for the return trip. He and the little girl made their way back, safe and sound.

As soon as the bike's front wheel hit the safety of land again, the crowd began cheering. "It's a miracle!" some cried. "You're safe!" They gathered around the little girl to hug her.

"What made you go with George?" an older woman asked the girl. "Weren't you afraid?"

"No, I wasn't afraid," the girl answered. "You see, I don't just believe in him — *I trust him.* He's my daddy."

There are two primary forces in this world, fear and faith. Fear can move you to destructiveness or sickness or failure. Only in rare instances will it motivate you to accomplishment. But faith is a greater force. Faith can drive itself into your consciousness and set you free from fear forever.

~Norman Vincent Peale, minister and author

Fear imprisons, faith liberates; ✓

fear paralyzes, faith empowers;

fear disheartens, faith encourages;

fear sickens, faith heals;

fear makes useless,

faith makes serviceable.

~ Harry Emerson Fosdick, Protestant clergyman

Kathryn, Cancer, and God

I called my friend Sam Beasley to complain about the injustice: "I just got word that my friend Kathryn has been diagnosed with stage four pancreatic cancer. She's only 68 years old. She's been sober for 30 years; she hasn't had a cigarette in 29 years; and she hasn't eaten sugar for 28 years. She flosses after every meal and her teeth are perfect. She's trim and athletic. She and her husband go biking every weekend. Their summer vacations are biking across Europe with friends. She's done everything right and still — still she gets cancer!"

"So, let me ask you a question," Sam said. "Are you her Higher Power? Are you her God?"

"Well, no."

"But what you're telling me is that you want to overrule her Higher Power," Sam said. "You think *you* know what's right for Kathryn."

"Uh . . ."

"For all we know, this might just be the best year of her life!" Sam said.

"Oh. I hadn't thought of it like that."

"Most people don't," Sam continued. "In fact, your friend Kathryn probably isn't thinking about it like that either. But the truth is, we don't know that the cancer just might come bearing gifts . . . and that this last year of her life might very well be the best."

Could Sam be right? Kathryn had expressed many worries, concerns, and complaints over the ten years that I knew her. Chief among them was the absence of an exit strategy from the high-stress business she owned. She often complained that her husband John was not sufficiently sensitive to her emotional needs. She said she felt lonely much of the time and had no close friends. And she fretted about her two daughters: Chloe was overweight and Dianne wasn't interested in getting married. Kathryn lamented the lack of grandchildren. Clearly, hers wasn't the picture-perfect family Kathryn thought it ought to be.

Underlying her concerns and complaints was a chronic refrain of fear and mistrust. Kathryn said she had a hard time trusting people. Myriad fears haunted her daily life: fear that her business wasn't making enough money, fear that she'd miss a deadline or make a mistake; fear of what others thought of her; fear of abandonment; fears for her daughters' happiness . . . her fears seemed endless.

To any outside observer, these worries seemed baseless and irrational. Kathryn was a wealthy woman with a long marriage to a handsome, successful man; she had two lovely homes; she leased a new Mercedes every three years; her daughters were talented, attractive, and smart; and her family enjoyed a lifestyle anyone would envy. But the fears were still there — they had nothing to do with objective conditions.

Within the first week of her diagnosis, all that began to change. Kathryn's husband took a leave of absence from his work and devoted himself to caring for her. He moved her business out of their home and put it up for sale while she was in the hospital, so when she came home all she had to do was focus on her health.

When I went to visit her in the hospital, I expected to find her crying and fearful — her usual response to anything bad. But the Kathryn who greeted me from her hospital bed was relaxed and glowing. Her room was filled with flowers, cards, and balloons. Her entire family was gathered there with her — her husband John, her daughters Chloe and Dianne, her sister Suzanne, and Suzanne's fiancé. Kathryn was basking in their love and attention. She told me that she felt peaceful and serene, trusting God that all would be well.

For the next seven months, Kathryn's life looked like the solar system — with Kathryn as the sun — and family and friends orbiting around her. She received calls and visitors daily. John doted on her. Chloe was at the house every day and Kathryn's sister Suzanne came frequently, too. Dianne got married, and Kathryn rallied to participate in the wedding. The happy couple got pregnant, fulfilling one of Kathryn's fondest wishes —

for a grandchild. With her business gone, Kathryn had the time and money to do anything she wanted — with her devoted husband by her side. They went on outings to the local arboretum and gardens, museums, movies, and their weekend home up the coast.

I think back on what my friend Sam had told me: This might very well be the best year of Kathryn's life. From all appearances, it was. Her cares and concerns of previous years simply disappeared — along with the fear that had gripped her. Her final months were filled with love, laughter, lively conversations, companionship, holidays and special occasions with her family, and treasured moments with loving friends. Kathryn got everything she'd ever wanted.

As is often the way with us humans, Kathryn finally realized that much of what she thought was missing had actually been there all along. In the words of the French writer Colette: "What a wonderful life I've had! I only wish I'd realized it sooner."

Cancer had come into Kathryn's life — bearing gifts. Best of these were the gifts of serenity and peace of mind.

Faith is not a storm cellar to which

men and women can flee for refuge

from the storms of life.

It is, instead, an inner force

that gives them the strength

to face those storms and their consequences

with serenity of spirit.

~ Samuel James Ervin Jr.,
former U.S. Senator from North Carolina

Surrender makes you . . .

F
Answered Prayers
A
I
T
H
F
U
L
L

I asked for wisdom . . .

    and God gave me problems to solve.

I asked for prosperity . . .

    and God gave me brains and the strength to work.

I asked for courage . . .

    and God gave me danger to overcome.

I asked for love . . .

    and God gave me troubled people to help.

I asked for favors . . .

    and God gave me opportunities.

I received nothing I wanted.

I received everything I needed.

My Prayer has been answered.

~ anonymous (Islamic origin)

Saved from Myself

I never thought it could happen to me.

How many thousands of times had I seen TV shows and movies in which someone is handcuffed, stuffed into the back of a cop car, and hauled off to jail? I'd seen it in real life a few times, too — it happens in L.A. — some hapless junkie arrested for trying to rob a 7-Eleven, a gangbanger busted for dealing dope, ladies of the night locked up for plying their trade. It happens, all right — to other people — not to me.

Yet here I was, in the middle of the night, handcuffed, sitting on the cold curb of a deserted street. "This can't be happening," I thought as I overheard the staccato voices and static coming from the police cruiser's radio. It was like something out of the *Twilight Zone*. I must have slipped through a time warp and entered some alternative reality. Perhaps I had made a wrong turn and walked onto a movie set where I was mistakenly caught up in the action. I felt disoriented and confused — in an alien world.

The cop got me to my feet, walked me to his black-and-white, and put his hand on my head as he assisted me into the backseat. "I don't belong here," I wept. "I'm a soccer mom, for God's sake. I'm somebody's mother. I'm as wholesome as Doris Day and apple pie. I'm not drunk — I'm just tired. There must be some mistake!"

How did I ever end up here?

Truth be told, I asked for this. Just twenty-four hours earlier I had been on my knees — sobbing at my bedside: "Please, God, help me. I can't stop drinking. Please stop me . . . " I drunkenly mumbled the Serenity Prayer and tumbled into bed.

And now, as the nice officers in the black-and-white car drove me to jail, I knew that my prayer had been answered — just not quite the way I had hoped. I stopped protesting and started praying. Bowing my head for a quiet conversation with God, I whispered: "Okay, God, I get it. You answered my prayer . . . but this isn't quite what I had in mind. The jig is up. My drinking days are done. I get the message."

It was an expensive adventure . . . and humiliating. I surrendered to the cops; I surrendered to God; and I surrendered the booze. I haven't had a drink since that night, so I figure God knew exactly what would do the trick. A cosmic 2-by-4 across the forehead — in the form of jail — got my attention, all right!

I asked for help, and He sent the cavalry in a squad car to save me. God always takes better care of me than I do of myself.

Some people change their ways

when they see the light,

others when they feel the heat.

~ Caroline Schoeder,
German-American pianist

I try not to micromanage my Higher Power.

I simply pray for what I want and need,

then let God decide how best to deliver it.

~ Sam Beasley, author

He knows what He is doing with me.
I cannot always understand His way,
but I am content in the realization
that He knows what is best.
That is surrender.

~Sri Daya Mata,
president of the Self-Realization Fellowship

God often takes a course for accomplishing
His purposes directly contrary to what
our narrow views would prescribe.
He brings a death upon our feelings, wishes,
and prospects when He is about to give us
the desire of our hearts.

~ John Newton, Anglican clergyman,
author of the hymn "Amazing Grace"

Surrender makes you . . .

FAITHFULL

Inspired by Grace

Don't seek God in temples.

He is close to you. He is within you.

Only you should surrender to Him

and you will rise above happiness

and unhappiness.

~ Leo Tolstoy, Russian author

✓ **The place where God can be found**

is the place where one stands.

~ Martin Buber, Jewish theologian

Grace

Grace, *noun: 1. The exercise of love, kindness, mercy, favor, disposition to benefit or serve another; favor bestowed or privilege conferred. 2. The divine favor toward man; the mercy of God, as distinguished from His justice; also, any benefits His mercy imparts; divine love or pardon; a state of acceptance with God; enjoyment of the divine favor.*

(Merriam-Webster)

Reading theology in graduate school nearly drove me to a nervous breakdown. I read one theologian after another, in a desperate search for the "right" understanding of God and the "truth" about how to live a good life. Each book offered answers that made sense . . . until I read the next book. Then I would be filled with confusion and despair. "Who's right?" I cried. Many a night I fell asleep on a pillow damp from tears of frustration, surrounded by theology texts. My faith was important to me — and I wanted to get it right.

At one point, my boyfriend Ron became so concerned about my distress that he suggested I drop my theology classes and pick another field of study. "Religion is supposed to make you feel better, not worse," he said. Right he was.

Finally, I did give up theology. "A pox on all their houses!" I denounced and renounced. "Those theologians — they're just a bunch of dead European white guys. What makes them think they've got the answers to the Big Questions of Life? God is too huge, too profound, too complex for a puny human brain to comprehend. It's *pure hubris* to think you can 'explain' God — or lay out a systematic theology. I'm done reading those guys. They're just spinning their wheels, debating how many angels can dance on the head of a pin! Phooey on them!"

Free at last, free at last, thank God Almighty, I felt free at last! I realized that I didn't need to "understand" God to love Him. There was no possible way to wrap my brain around the enormity of Cosmic Consciousness — so I wasn't going to try. I would content myself with the *experience* of Divine Presence in my daily life. I could feel God at work and that reassured me. Occasional glimpses of the Numinous filled me with awe and wonder . . . and that was better than any theology.

However, my theology studies were not a complete waste. I did come away with one very useful concept, and that is: *"As a spiritual person, how do I live my life in response to the gift of Grace?"* Of everything I read, it was the notion that made the most sense. It is a simple concept — though not always easy to put into practice. It is both inspirational and practical. I think it is *the* central question for anyone seeking to live a surrendered, faith-full life.

Faith is not something to grasp; it is a state to grow into.

~ Gandhi, India's spiritual leader, father of Indian independence

Faith doesn't wait until it understands; in that case it wouldn't be faith.

·· Erich Fromm, German-born psychoanalyst

I've discovered there are only two modes of the heart. We can struggle, or we can surrender. Surrender is a frightening word for some people, because it might be interpreted as passivity, or timidity. Surrender means wisely accommodating ourselves to what is beyond our control. Getting old, getting sick, dying, losing what is dear to us, what the Buddha taught as the first Noble Truth, or life's unsatisfactoriness — is beyond our control. I can either be frightened of life and mad at life — or not. I can be disappointed and still not be mad. Stopping being mad — when I can — translates, for me, as being compassionate — to myself and to other people.

~ Sylvia Boorstein, psychotherapist, Buddhist teacher, and observant Jew

Living Loving Kindness

"My religion is kindness,"
  the holy man says.

His almond eyes crinkle
as he smiles.
Wisdom is etched in the lines
of his beautiful brown face.

He bows
    and calls himself
        "a simple monk."

My heart feels calm and peaceful
    In his presence.

He is, indeed, living loving kindness.

♥ ♥

"Be the living expression
of God's kindness,"
        the wise old woman says.
"Kindness in your face,
        kindness in your eyes,
                kindness in your smile."
Some call her
        the "goddess of kindness."

Her weathered face
glows with love
        as she washes the feet
        of a dying beggar.
He is soothed by the touch
        of her strong, gnarled hands.

She is, indeed, living loving kindness.

♥ ♥

"Do your little bit of good
while you are here,"
        the magnificent black man says.
"It's those little bits of good
        put together
                that overwhelm the world."

He is a small man
        with a huge presence.

He throws his arms open wide,
and declares:
"God has a dream —
of a place where we are all
members of one family
God's family."

This man of truth and reconciliation
is, indeed, living loving kindness.

♥ ♥

There are saints among us —

    saints of kindness and compassion —

    the simple monk of Tibet,

    the saint of the gutter in Calcutta,

    the holy man of South Africa.

They all preach the same gospel —

    the gospel of living loving kindness.

If asked to explain,

    each would simply say,

        "My life is my message."

There are, indeed, saints among us.

♥ ♥ ♥ ♥

Buddha said that fortune changes like the swish of a horse's tail. Tomorrow could be the first day of thirty years of quadriplegia. . . . The more you open to life, the less death becomes the enemy. When you start using death as a means of focusing on life, then everything becomes just as it is, just this moment, an extraordinary opportunity to be really alive.

~ Stephen Levine, poet,
spiritual teacher, author

Life Is a Cookie

One of my patients, a successful businessman, tells
me that before his cancer he would become depressed
unless things went a certain way. Happiness was
"having the cookie." If you had the cookie, things were
good. If you didn't have the cookie, life wasn't worth a
darn. Unfortunately, the cookie kept changing. Some
of the time it was money . . . . At other times, it was
the new car, the biggest contract, the most prestigious
address. A year and a half [later] . . . he sits shaking
his head ruefully. "It's like I stopped learning how to
live after I was a kid. When I give my son a cookie, he
is happy. If I take the cookie away or it breaks, he is
unhappy. But he is two-and-a-half and I am forty-three.
It's taken me this long to understand that the cookie
will never make me happy for long. The minute you
have the cookie it starts to crumble or you start to
worry about it crumbling or about someone trying to
take it away from you. You know, you have to give up a
lot of things to take care of the cookie, to keep it from
crumbling and be sure that no one takes it away from
you. You may not even get a chance to eat it because
you are so busy just trying not to lose it. Having the
cookie is not what life is about."

My patient laughs and says cancer has changed him. For the first time, he is happy. No matter if his business is doing well or not, no matter if he wins or loses at golf. "Two years ago, cancer asked me, 'Okay, what is important? What is really important?' Well, life is important. Life. Life any way you can have it. Life with the cookie, life without the cookie. Happiness does not have anything to do with the cookie, it has to do with being alive. Before, who made the time?" He pauses thoughtfully. "Damn, I guess life is the cookie."

~ Rachel Naomi Remen, MD,
author, medical reformer, educator

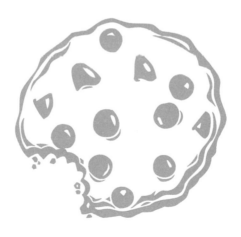

This is the precious present, regardless of what yesterday was like, regardless of what tomorrow may bring.

When your inner eyes open, you can find immense beauty hidden within the inconsequential details of daily life.

When your inner ears are open, you can hear the subtle, lovely music of the universe everywhere you go.

When the heart of your heart opens, you can take deep pleasure in the company of the people around you — family, friends, acquaintances, or strangers — including those whose characters are less than perfect, just as your character is less than perfect.

When you are open to the beauty, mystery, and grandeur of ordinary existence, you "get it," that it always has been beautiful, mysterious, and grand and always will be.

~ Timothy Miller, PhD,
author and psychologist

How to Build a Life

- Build your life on the firm foundation of true gratitude to God for all His blessings and true humility because of your unworthiness of these blessings.

- Build the frame of your life out of self-discipline; never let yourself get selfish or lazy or contented with yourself.

- Build the walls of your life out of service to others, helping them to find the way to live.

- Build the roof of your life out of prayer and quiet times, waiting for God's guidance from above.

- Build a garden around your life out of peace of mind and serenity and a sure faith.

~ Twenty-Four Hours a Day (published by Hazelden)

Surrender makes you . . .

FAITH

Trust in Divine Guidance

To wait open-endedly is an enormously radical attitude toward life. So is to trust that something will happen to us that is far beyond our imaginings. So, too, is giving up control over our future and letting God define our life, trusting that God moulds us according to God's love and not according to our fear. The spiritual life is a life in which we wait, actively present to the moment, trusting that new things will happen to us, new things that are far beyond our own imagination, fantasy, or prediction. That, indeed, is a very radical stance toward life in a world preoccupied with control.

~ Henri J.M. Nouwen, Belgian Catholic mystic

A New Employer

Like many companies over the past ten years, the
company that I worked for in Los Angeles was
downsizing — offering buyout packages as an incentive
for employees to leave the company. What a great deal!
I had been unhappy in my job for quite some time,
and this looked like the perfect escape. My severance
package would provide a modest financial cushion for
me to start a business of my own. I was nervous about
leaving the security of a big corporation, especially since
I was single and over 40, and the country was in the
midst of a recession. To say that I was concerned would
be an understatement.

I've been told that one should have enough money
to live on for two years when you start a new business,
and I only had enough to last about nine months.
But still, it was a start. My concern was mixed with
excitement and anticipation.

I set up my home office in the basement and ordered
inexpensive business cards and stationery from my local
Kinko's. I bought a fax machine and a computer. I made
up a list of several business ideas — the kinds of things I
thought I'd like to do. I was ready to begin.

As the weeks rolled by, I spent my time doing
research on my list of business ideas. I would do

interviews with entrepreneurs and ask them questions about their businesses. I read books and trade journals. I read the *Wall Street Journal* and magazines for entrepreneurs. I pursued each of my ideas with thorough research and dogged determination.

One by one, I explored each of the ideas on my list. And one by one, I crossed them off the list, as each one turned out to be not right for me.

As the weeks turned into months, my list of possible business ideas got shorter and shorter, and I got more and more discouraged. It seems each idea led me down a blind alley to a dead end. I was running out of ideas — my fear and dread grew stronger. What was I going to do?

Finally the day came when I had exhausted my list of ideas. None of them had worked out, nine months had gone by, and I was almost out of money. I was terrified.

I woke up one morning, sat on the edge of my bed, bowed my head, and began to pray:

"Well, God, you had better tell me what to do because I am absolutely clueless. I don't have the first idea of how to start a business, or even what business to go into. I'm turning my career and my future over to you, because I don't know what to do. God, I'm putting *you* in charge of my career and my business — from now on, *you're* the boss."

I got dressed and went about my household chores and errands . . .

As I went through my day, a simple question softly made its way into my awareness. "What are your gifts?" the gentle voice asked.

Stopping my activity to engage in conversation with this still, small voice, I thought for a minute and then replied, "My gifts are teaching and writing."

"Then do that," the gentle voice said. It was as simple as that. The conversation was over. A quiet peacefulness came over me. The fear was gone; I felt clear and calm. I had a mission.

The next morning, my phone rang, and a woman's voice on the other end asked me if I would be interested in designing a new employee orientation program for her company. This woman had known me when I was the training manager for the company that had given me the severance package. She knew the quality of my work and had called the old company to get my phone number. We had a short conversation, made an appointment to meet and discuss details, and then hung up the phone.

I got on my knees and began to pray — this time a prayer of thanks. I had a new employer. I finally knew who was *really* going to run my business, and my mission was clear: I would teach and write, making my contribution to people's lives through the seminars that I lead and the books that I write. With my mind and heart finally open to divine guidance, all fear went away, and I knew I was in business.

Prayer is surrender — surrender to the will of God and cooperation with that will. If I throw out a boathook from the boat and catch hold of the shore and pull, do I pull the shore to me, or do I pull myself to the shore? Prayer is not pulling God to my will, but the aligning of my will to the will of God.

~ E. Stanley Jones,
Methodist missionary, theologian

Many people are using personal-power instead of God-power, which always brings unhappy reaction. Personal-power means forcing personal will. . . . Man controls conditions by a knowledge of Spiritual law.

~ Florence Scovel Shinn,
American artist and illustrator and
metaphysical writer

We must be willing to let go of

the life we have planned,

so as to have the life that is waiting for us.

~ E. M. Forster

Let go...

Few souls understand what God would

accomplish in them if they were to abandon

themselves unreservedly to Him and if they were

to allow His grace to mould them accordingly.

~ St. Ignatius Loyola

Power Source

God is like electricity.

I can't see electricity
        but I know it's real
                because I see its results.
Electricity lights up my home,
        makes my appliances work,
                and powers my computer.

God is like that.

I can't see God but
        I know He's real
                because I see His results.
God creates life,
        makes the planets spin in orbit,
                and powers my body and mind.

I don't doubt the existence of electricity
        just because it's invisible —
nor do I doubt God
        just because He's invisible.

I wouldn't try to operate my computer

       without plugging it into a power source.

Why would I try to run *my life*

       without tapping into a power source?

Without faith, nothing is possible.

With it, nothing is impossible.

~ Mary McLeod Bethune, civil rights activist

God's Money

A couple of years ago I was having a hard time financially. It had been a slow year for business; I'd had some big medical bills; and I had not been as careful with my money as I should have been. It was November, and I didn't know how I was going to make it through the end of the year. I called my friend Anna to ask her advice. She had a good head for money.

I tearfully explained my predicament. She listened quietly. She was kind and sympathetic. She did not judge or scold. "You want my advice?" she asked, when I had finished telling her my sad story.

"Well, sure," I replied, "that's why I called you."

"Tithe," she said simply.

I couldn't believe my ears. "You don't understand," I objected. "I just told you — I don't have any money coming in, I've got all these bills piled up, and I don't know how I'm going to meet the mortgage next month. I can't tithe — I have nothing to tithe with!"

"Well, you asked my advice, and I'm giving it to you," she said matter-of-factly. "All I have to share with you is my own experience. If you start to tithe, you shift your relationship with God. It is an act of faith in which you essentially say, 'I know I will be taken care of, so I can give this money back to God.' It works for me, and it works for lots of other people I know, too."

I knew in my heart of hearts that Anna was right. Tithing was something I had wanted to do for a long time, but I was afraid — afraid I would not have enough money to meet my needs, afraid to give away 10% of my income, afraid of financial insecurity. I had heard other people talk about tithing in the past, and being a spiritual person, I liked the idea — but my fear always got the better of me.

"Here's what I'd suggest," Anna continued, "Why don't you call Naomi and ask her what her experience has been with tithing. Call Constance, too, and see what she has to say. Then decide if it's right for you."

I thanked Anna for her advice, and immediately dialed Naomi's number. She was more than happy to tell me about her experience with tithing. Anna had given her the same advice she'd given me. Reluctantly, Naomi agreed to do it. She started by tithing to a 12-step group, because Anna had instructed her to "give to the spiritual community that nurtures you." Naomi took a check to the office of this 12-step program every time she got paid (she was self-employed in the real estate business). "The first time I tithed," Naomi told me, "I sold a $400,000 house the very next week! I made a great commission."

After a while, Anna suggested that Naomi start tithing to her local synagogue, since she had been born and raised Jewish. Naomi protested. "I lost my faith years ago, and I'm not going to give them any money." Anna nudged Naomi, "Just try it. See what happens." So the next time Naomi got paid, she drove to the synagogue and gave them a check. Before long, the rabbi invited her to come to a special event at the synagogue. She went. She met a few people she liked and started going to more events. Her heart began softening toward the faith she had rejected, and over time she gradually felt more a part of this community. Finally, Naomi became an official member of the temple.

About this time, her nephew turned 13, and it was time for him to have his bar mitzvah. Naomi had been estranged from her sister, but she loved her nephew very much, and she wanted to pay for the bar mitzvah. Over the months of planning the event, Naomi and her sister gradually worked through their differences and were reconciled.

In short, Naomi's commitment to tithe 10 percent of whatever she earned transformed her life. Tithing did more than put her on sound financial ground — it brought her back to her faith, and it reunited her with her sister. She was living a life of miracles.

If I had any doubt about the efficacy of tithing, it disappeared in listening to Naomi's story. Tithing means acknowledging that no matter how little one has, there are always other people who are worse off. Tithing means saying to God, "I trust that You will provide for me, and I am willing to give back 10 percent to do Your work in the world." Tithing lifts the burden of fear from my heart and replaces it with trust. Tithing to a spiritual organization that gives me spiritual sustenance is the best way of saying "thanks" for all that I have received.

I once heard Jack Canfield (coauthor of *Chicken Soup for the Soul*) talk about tithing and its role in his life. He said, "Both my coauthor and I have been tithing for many years, and we think it's an important part of our business success. (Their *Chicken Soup* books have sold more than 80 million copies!) But I have to tell you, it was a lot easier to write those checks in the early years, when they were smaller. It's kind of hard to sit down today and write tithing checks for $100,000!" I laughed when he said that. That's a problem I'd *love* to have!

I've been tithing for several years now, ever since the phone conversations I had with Anna and Naomi. I don't sell real estate, and I haven't had the success of *Chicken Soup*, but my finances have stabilized and the peace of mind I feel is wonderful.

Tithing shifted my relationship to God from one of a fearful child asking God's protection . . . to one of a willing partner with God in doing His work in the world. Best of all, I discovered something I never would have seen if I hadn't surrendered and let go of my financial fears: *The best things in life aren't things.*

Surrender makes you . . .

FAITH

Humble Service and Contribution

**Life's most persistent
and urgent question is:
"What are you doing for others?"**

~ Rev. Martin Luther King Jr.

**What do we live for,
if it is not to make life
less difficult for each other?**

~ George Eliot

Give 'Til It Hurts ✓

Reverend Ed Bacon of All Saints Episcopal Church in
Pasadena, California, stood in his pulpit, resplendent
in his flowing white robe and colorful vestments. He's
a big man with a booming voice and charisma enough
to light up the sanctuary without candles. On this
particular Sunday, he was practically glowing with
joy — energized by his guest of honor, Archbishop
Desmond Tutu, the Nobel Prize winning peacemaker
from South Africa.

"Most people say, 'Give 'til it hurts,'" Reverend Ed
announced to the standing-room-only congregation.
"But I say, 'Give 'til it feels good!'"

The crowd's laughter and applause thundered their
approval. The choir burst into song as ushers made their
way down the aisles with collection baskets.

This wasn't just any Sunday — and it wasn't just any
collection. Archbishop Tutu had come to All Saints to
tell us about the latest developments in his homeland.
Apartheid had been abolished, and the country was now
embarking on the long, slow, painful journey of healing.
A Truth and Reconciliation Commission (TRC) had
been established to facilitate the healing process. It was
a court-like body, chaired by Archbishop Tutu, which

played a key role in the transition of South Africa to a full and free democracy. Anyone who felt that he or she had been a victim of apartheid's violence could come forward and be heard. Perpetrators of violence could also give testimony and request amnesty and forgiveness.

But, as Reverend Ed pointed out to us that Sunday morning, justice isn't free. It costs money to hold tribunals, to handle the paperwork, to underwrite the process of hearings and all the administrative details. So he asked the congregation to dig deep into our pockets and purses, since he was giving all the donations that Sunday to Archbishop Tutu to help support the ongoing work of the Truth and Reconciliation Commission.

"I've never done this before," Reverend Ed said, "But I'm going to do it today. I am urging you to give what you can, in whatever form you can. If you want to donate your car, we'll take the pink slip. If you want to donate jewelry, we'll take that. If you want to give cash or a check, or even put your donation on a credit card, fine. We'll take it all. We here in Southern California have a wonderful standard of living — we're rich by any standard. So I'm asking you to give as much as you can to the people of South Africa to support their healing and reconciliation. Most people say, 'Give until it hurts' — but I say, *'Give until it feels good!'*"

There wasn't a dry eye in the place. We were so moved by Tutu's sermon, so inspired by his moral authority and loving compassion, that we could do no less than give our all.

As the collection basket made its way toward me, I wondered what to do. My business had been slow, so I had no extra money to give. I needed my car, so I couldn't donate that. *What can I give?* I asked myself. I desperately wanted to support this marvelous process unfolding in South Africa. I wanted to contribute something — no matter how small — to the good people halfway around the world.

The collection basket finally came to me, and I looked down into it, still not sure what to do. As my hands cradled the basket of love offerings, I noticed that I was wearing a 14K gold and garnet ring my mother had given me on my twelfth birthday. Instantly, I knew what to do. I took off the ring, put it in the little white offering envelope, and dropped the envelope into the collection basket. Tears of joy streamed down my face as I passed the basket to the person next to me. I imagined the South Africans melting down my gold ring to help pay for their national healing. I was filled with gratitude and happiness to be a tiny part of something so momentous, so important, so essential to humanity.

As I wiped away my tears and joined the choir in song, I realized that Reverend Ed had been right. I gave . . . and it felt good.

**A check or credit card, a Gucci bag strap,
anything of value will do. Give as you live.**

~ Rev. Jesse Jackson, civil rights leader

Keep yourself like an empty vessel for God to fill. Keep pouring out yourself to help others so that God can keep filling you up with His spirit. The more you give, the more you will have for yourself. God will see that you are kept filled as long as you are giving to others. But if you selfishly try to keep all for yourself, you are soon blocked off from God, your source of supply, and you will become stagnant. To be clear, a lake must have an inflow and an outflow.

~ Twenty-Four Hours a Day (Anonymous, pub. by Hazelden)

**All who joy would win must share it.
Happiness was born a twin.**

~ Lord Byron, English poet

Giving

"It's better to give than receive,"
        my mother used to say.
But it took some years
        of experience
before I fully understood
what she meant.

When I gave my subway seat
to an old lady,
        I felt kind.

When I dropped a dollar
into the street musician's hat,
        I felt generous.

When I let the harried driver
cut in front of me on the road,
        I felt patient.

When I lent a hand
to someone at work,
        I felt a part of the team.

When I brought a meal
to my grieving neighbor,
        I felt empathetic.

When I gave some water
to a thirsty dog,
        I felt happy.

When I wrote a check
to a worthy cause,
        I felt virtuous.

When I gave my friend
the benefit of the doubt,
        I felt compassionate.

I discovered that
when I give my time,
        my attention,
        my money,
        my thoughtfulness
to another —

                I feel wonderful.

Mom was right . . .
it IS better to give
than receive.

In giving,
we generate warmth;
in giving,
we feel connected;
in giving,
we discover love.

Kindness

in words creates confidence.

Kindness in thinking creates profoundness.

Kindness in giving creates love.

~ Lao Tzu, Chinese philosopher

How to lend a HELPING HAND . . .

Hearing what's needed

Eager to contribute

Listening with compassion

Paying attention to the little things

Intuitively understanding what's helpful and what's not

Never overstepping your bounds

Going out of your way for a true friend

Healing love, healing touch

Asking "What can I do to help?"

Never assuming that you know what's best

Desiring to serve and contribute to others' well-being

Peace Prayer of St. Francis

Lord, make me an instrument of Your peace:
Where there is hatred, let me sow love;
where there is injury, pardon;
where there is doubt, faith;
where there is despair, hope;
where there is darkness, light;
and where there is sadness, joy.

O, Divine Master:
Grant that I may not so much seek
to be consoled as to console;
to be understood as to understand;
to be loved as to love.
For it is in giving that we receive;
it is in pardoning that we are pardoned;
and it is in dying to ourselves that we are born to eternal life.

Surrender makes you . . .

FAITHFULL

Freedom from Ego

Angels can fly because

they take themselves lightly.

~ G.K. Chesterton, English writer

EGO = *Edging God Out*

This is a tale of two *Today Shows*.

A couple years ago, a *Today Show* producer called to invite me to come on the show for a segment about women breaking up with their girlfriends. I told almost no one I was going; I just went to New York and did the show.

I felt serene and peaceful as I said a little prayer before it was my turn to go on the set with Matt Lauer. "God, give the words that might help the women who are watching this show today, and perhaps struggling with painful friendships." The segment went smoothly, and I had a great time. As I left the set, the executive producer approached and asked for my card. "I just love your energy!" she enthused. I told her the segment producer had my card and contact information.

The next day I flew home, happy with my excursion to the Big Apple. I felt good about my contribution to the show.

A few weeks later, another producer from the *Today Show* called and asked me to come back for a segment on bad bosses. But this time I reacted differently. I got excited. I sent out an e-mail blast, telling all my friends, family, and business contacts that I was going on the show.

I called an author friend with a lot of TV experience and asked for his advice. "Take charge of the interview," he said. "And be sure to take a copy of your book with you."

I obsessed about what to wear. I hauled several outfits to a neighbor's house and tried them all on, soliciting advice about which one was best. I borrowed special jewelry to wear on the show. And I made notes about what I wanted to say — *pages* of notes!

The day arrived when I was to fly to New York, and it seemed as if it was jinxed from the get-go. Everything that could go wrong, did go wrong. The executive producer came backstage to greet me. She threw open her arms to hug me as if we were lifetime friends. Her hair was different; her outfit was different; and I thought she was Sarah Jessica Parker. "Do I know you?" I asked quizzically. Wrong move.

Then, when it was my turn to go onto the set for my segment, I took a copy of my book with me to give to the interviewer while we were on camera. The same executive producer strode across the stage, snatched it from my hands, and scolded, "Don't ever bring a book onto this set! Not if you want to be invited back. It's tacky." She turned and threw the book across the set. Oh god, I knew I was in trouble for sure.

A new guy was substituting for Matt Lauer, and he seemed nervous and fidgety — perhaps eager to do a good job filling in for the hugely popular Lauer. Cameras rolled and the new guy introduced me — misreading the title of my book as he worked from the teleprompter. My heart sank. The interview went badly. The new guy was hurried and awkward — he stepped all over my lines. I felt off balance through the whole thing. When our segment ended and I left the set, my heart was down in my shoes. I felt the whole thing had been a disaster.

I flew home from New York the next day feeling disappointed, dejected, and humiliated. I knew they would never invite me back.

What was the difference between the two shows? Pretty obvious: the difference was *me*. I got in my own way. Instead of showing up to be of service to viewers, I got caught up in looking good and self-promotion. My ego tried to run the show, and it made a mess of everything.

I learned a painful lesson. And still today, whenever I recall the executive producer scolding me on the set, I can feel the sting of embarrassment. Ouch.

But in some ways, I hope I never forget that "ouch" . . . because it reminds me to keep my ego out of the way. When I show up in service to others, things always go perfectly. When I show up strutting my stuff, I make a mess of things.

Who knows? Perhaps that executive producer was a spiritual messenger sent to tell me to "cut the crap." If so, I want to say, "Thanks, I needed that."

When your work speaks for itself,

don't interrupt.

~ Henry J. Kaiser, industrialist and shipbuilder

Humility does not mean thinking less of yourself than other people, nor does it mean having a low opinion of your own gifts. It means freedom from thinking about yourself at all.

~ William Temple, Archbishop of Canterbury

We should take care not to make

the intellect our God.

~ Albert Einstein

*My mind can easily get in my way. It tries to be logical.
It figures out problems and thinks it has answers. Then my
life becomes chaotic. It is only when I let go and let God
that I feel serenity. It is only when I give up that I see the
answers God puts before me. It is only when I stop trying
to control that my life runs smoothly.*

*God runs my life better than I do. I must remember to stay
out of the way.*

~from For Today (O.A.)

You have to become Somebody
before you can become nobody.

~ Ram Dass, spiritual teacher

To pray is to pay attention to something
or someone other than oneself.
Whenever a man so concentrates his attention
— on a landscape, a poem, a geometrical
problem, an idol, or the True God —that he
completely forgets his own ego and desires,
he is praying.

~ W.H. Auden, English poet

The Path

Love tells me I am everything.
Wisdom tells me I am nothing.
And between the two my life flows.

Buddha said,
"Take the Middle Way."

Easier said than done.

Character

A wise Buddhist master once told me, "When you are considering someone to be your guru or teacher, first go for a ride with him in his car. That will tell you much about whether or not he is the right person for you."

I have thought of that cautionary insight many times, when I have passengers in my car:

- Am I patient and calm while driving?

- How do I behave when I'm stuck in gridlock traffic?

- Am I quick to anger when someone cuts in front of me?

- Is my driving sensible and safe . . . or am I reckless behind the wheel?

- Am I mindful in each moment, paying full attention to my driving?

- Is my ego driving the car . . . asserting *my way or the highway*?

- Am I compassionate in dealing with other drivers?

🍂 Am I grateful . . . for my car which carries me without complaint, for the highways that enable me to travel quickly, for the road maintenance crews who keep my journey smooth and safe, and for the other drivers who are my fellow travelers on Life's journey?

I have to ask myself, "Would anyone choose *me* to be their guru or teacher, based on how I conduct myself behind the wheel?"

Traffic doesn't determine character — it reveals it.

This is the true joy in life:

. . . being used for a purpose recognized by
yourself as a mighty one;

. . . being thoroughly worn out before you are
thrown on the scrap heap;

. . . being a force of nature instead of a feverish
selfish little clod of ailments and grievances
complaining that the world will not devote itself
to making you happy.

~ George Bernard Shaw, Irish playwright

Give up all bad qualities in you;

banish the ego and develop

the spirit of surrender.

You will then experience Bliss.

~ Sri Sathya Sai Baba, South Indian spiritual teacher

Surrender makes you . . .

FAITHFULL

Unconditional Forgiveness

Holding on to a resentment is like swallowing

poison and hoping the other person will die.

~ anonymous

Daisies

My wise friend Jaime once told me the story of a young woman with a suitor who loved her very much. The suitor came to her door clutching a bouquet of daisies to give her. "Where are my roses?" she demanded. "I want roses." Her suitor turned and went away.

The next week he was back on her doorstep with another bunch of daisies. Upon seeing the flowers in his hand, the young woman said, "Where are my roses? I want roses." Again the suitor turned and went away.

The following week the same thing happened. The suitor showed up at his true love's door with a bunch of daisies. The young woman said, "Where are my roses? I want roses." And so again he left.

This went on for several more weeks, until finally one week, the suitor didn't come. And he never came to her door again.

Jaime explained to me that people love us in their own ways — but sometimes we don't recognize their love because it doesn't show up the way we think it should. Someone offers us daisies, but we keep insisting on roses. After a while, the person who loves us may stop showing up at all if we fail to recognize his love in the way he expresses it.

This parable isn't just for lovers — it's for anyone who wants to love and be loved. It's true of friends; it's true of siblings; it's true of parents and children.

I spent many years being angry and resentful with my parents — especially my dad — for the way they "didn't love me." Their structure and discipline felt cold and harsh. I wanted parents who doted on me. Their perfectionism made them seem impossible to please, though I tried mightily. I wanted parents who thought that *everything* I did was wonderful. Their carefulness with money felt unloving to me. I wanted parents who were generous to a fault. My parents kept giving me daisies, and I kept looking for roses.

I am embarrassed to admit that it took me many, many years to recognize the daisies for what they were — love. My parents loved me very much — and still do. It's just that their idea of how to be responsible parents was very different from what I had in mind. I wanted to be Daddy's little princess, but instead I felt like Cinderella being forced to do dirty chores, like cleaning the bathroom, washing dinner dishes, and babysitting my grubby brother.

My father was careful with money because he was a child of the Depression and he knew what it was like not to have enough food. He watched expenses like a hawk because he wanted to make sure that *his* children would never go hungry. He saved as much money as he possibly could, in case he died young — his children would not be farmed out to cousins, as he had been when his father died young. In short, my father had learned a hard kind of love — getting bounced around from family to family, to whoever could afford to feed him. He knew that children need to be taught important lessons right from the get-go, because life is harsh and you never know if the kids might be forced to fend for themselves. Dad was a military man who fought in three wars — so there was a very real chance that his career might make his wife a widow and his children orphans.

I am very fortunate that my parents are both still alive. And I'm fortunate that my friend Jaime taught me how to recognize the daisies for what they were — love in the only way my folks knew how to show it.

Most of all, I'm fortunate to have found forgiveness in my heart — forgiveness for all the ways I was hurt by my parents and forgiveness for myself for judging them so harshly for so long. I lost a lot of quality time with my family because I couldn't get past my resentments about the way they raised me.

I know countless people who are still nursing deep resentments toward their parents and carrying around mountains of emotional baggage from childhood. My heart goes out to them because I know how much they are still suffering — I was once one of them.

I am grateful that, through the grace of spiritual teachings and the help of some very wise friends, I was finally able to wake up and smell the daisies.

All the years you have waited for them to "make it up to you" and all the energy you expended trying to make them change (or make them pay) kept the old wounds from healing and gave pain from the past free rein to shape and even damage your life. And still they may not have changed. Nothing you have done has made them change. Indeed, they may never change. Inner peace is found by changing yourself, not the people who hurt you. And you change yourself for yourself — for the joy, serenity, peace of mind, understanding, compassion, laughter, and bright future that you get.

~ Rev. Lewis B. Smedes,
Reformed Church minister, author, and theologian

Blame your parents for the way you are

. . . blame yourself if you stay that way.

~ Mom

How do we practice
FORGIVENESS . . . ?

Feel your hurt.

Open your mind.

Release your anger.

Give love a chance.

Inquire within your heart.

Venture into dialogue.

Embrace the other person.

Nudge yourself to keep at it, even when you don't want to.

Enjoy new possibilities and freedom.

Seek Divine guidance and help.

Savor your new serenity and peace.

Love is the answer.

Love is the most healing force there is.

Love abolishes anger.

Love releases resentment.

Love gets rid of guilt.

Love banishes blame.

Love fades fear.

Love opens the door.

Love is the pathway to freedom and peace of mind.

Love is the answer . . .

and forgiveness is the way to love.

~ Louise Hay, spiritual teacher

Forgiveness is a funny thing.

It warms the heart and cools the sting.

~ William Arthur Ward, inspirational author

Guilt

Single parent guilt plagued me for many years. Having grown up watching family TV — *The Donna Reed Show*, *Leave it to Beaver*, and *Father Knows Best* — I carried in my head an ideal image of the perfect mother, and I knew I wasn't her. I fell so far short of the kind of mom I wanted to be that I was filled with guilt and remorse while I was raising my son, and it continued long after he was grown and gone from our home.

I felt guilty about everything — getting pregnant and giving birth while I was just a teenager, drinking while pregnant, ending my marriage within a few years, taking my son away from his father and moving across the country, being an inconsistent and unreliable caretaker, losing my temper and hitting my child, allowing my boyfriends to spend the night, working full-time and turning my son into a latchkey kid, and much more. I had plenty to feel bad about.

Over the years, acutely aware of my parental shortcomings, I tried to assuage my guilt in different ways — often compounding the problem. I used food to express love: "Here, I love you, eat." "Look what Mommy brought you from the restaurant where I went on my date." "Mommy is too 'tired' (code for drunk) to fix dinner tonight. Here's some money — call the pizza delivery and order whatever you want."

One afternoon, when Michael was six, I told him I was going to the market and asked if he wanted to come with me. "No, I want to stay home and watch TV," he replied. "Okay, I'll be home in a little while," I said as I left. On the way to the market I thought I'd make a quick stop at the bookstore and look for a book I'd been wanting to read. One thing led to another (it's been known to happen in bookstores) and the next thing you know, it was dusk and I still hadn't made it to the market. I rushed to buy the groceries I needed, then hurried home in the dark. I opened the door, and there was Michael, sitting on the sofa sobbing. "Where . . . have . . . you been?!" he choked out his words between sobs. "Oh, honey, I am so sorry," I apologized. "I stopped at the bookstore and lost track of time. The next thing you know, it was dark. I am *so* sorry." Then I reached into the grocery bag and pulled out a box of Fudgsicles. "Look, I brought you some Fudgsicles! Does that make it better?" "NO!" he replied. "Having *you* home makes it better!" I felt like I was two inches tall. What kind of horrible mother tries to buy off her kid with sweets?

Food wasn't the only thing I tried to use to assuage my guilt. Presents, too. I bought expensive guitars and amplifiers over the years, a big stereo TV for his room, and plenty of toys and art supplies. Somehow I fooled myself into thinking that if I could be a good material provider, it might make up for my lapses in being an emotional provider. But deep down inside, I wasn't really fooled at all.

Guilt was my constant companion.

Over the years, I've tried to purge my guilt with apologies to my son. But guilt is like quicksand; the harder I struggled to free myself, the deeper I sunk. Nothing worked; no conversation, no apology, no amends I tried to make to him could lift my burden.

The problem wasn't lack of forgiveness on my son's part — he forgave me long ago. In fact, there have been times in the course of our conversations when he would point out, "Mom, you've got this 'Bad Mom' story about yourself. When are you going to let that go? It's really getting old, you know?"

About five years ago, after I'd had yet another bout with the guilt, a spiritual advisor suggested that I write a letter to Michael, listing everything I felt guilty about as his mom. It was a moral inventory, if you will — a "bad mom" laundry list of all my failures and shortcomings. "When you're done writing the letter, call and read it to me," she instructed.

So I followed her suggestion and wrote the letter — pages and pages. Then I called her and read it over the phone, allowing the tears to come whenever they chose. When I finished reading, I asked, "Now, should I send it to Michael?"

"Absolutely not," she replied. "This letter was for you, not for him. The next thing to do is find a safe place to burn the letter and let the smoke carry your guilt and grief away. Say a little prayer as you do this, and ask God to grant you forgiveness and remove your guilt."

I did as she suggested. My sadness lifted, my grief subsided, and my guilt was gone. God had done for me what I had been unable to do for myself.

**I have never seen a person grow or change
in a self-constructive meaningful way when
motivated by guilt, shame, or self-hate.**

~ Herb Goldberg, therapist, author

*That great morning of forgiveness may not come
at once. Do not give up if at first you fail. Often
the most difficult part of repentance is to forgive
yourself. Discouragement is part of that test. Do
not give up. That brilliant morning will come.*

~ Boyd K. Packer, Mormon Elder

**When you forgive, you in no way change the past
— but you sure do change the future.**

~ Bernard Meltzer, radio host

Surrender makes you . . .

FAITHFULL

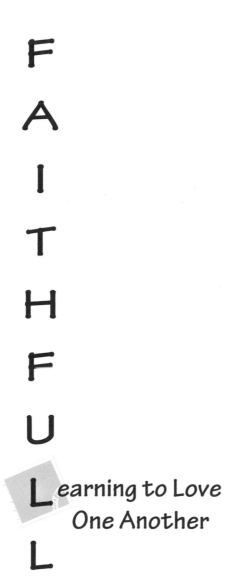

earning to Love One Another

I have learned silence from the talkative,

tolerance from the intolerant,

and kindness from the unkind;

yet, strange, I am ungrateful to those teachers.

~ Kahlil Gibran, Lebanese-American author

Other People

"Hell is other people," wrote the French existentialist philosopher, Jean-Paul Sartre. He was right, but only half right. The other half is, "Heaven is other people, too." Yes, it is our relationships with other people that give us most of our headaches, but relationships can also give us much joy.

Bankers can be overheard muttering, "This would be a great place to work, if it weren't for the customers." University people sometimes comment, "This would be a great place, if it weren't for the students." Record company executives love the music industry, but complain that the musicians are a pain in the ass. Book publishers occasionally gripe, "This would be a wonderful business, if only we didn't have to deal with pesky authors." In every workplace, there are troublesome people. Employees bitch about their bosses; bosses complain about their employees. Departments point the finger at each other. And customers blame everyone.

So you go home at the end of the day, hoping to find a little peace, quiet, understanding, love, and support. And what do you get? Whining kids, sulking teens, and/or a spouse who's had his or her own share of difficult people to deal with today.

Difficult people are everywhere — in neighborhoods, schools, hospitals, government, and yes, even in churches, temples, ashrams, monasteries, and mosques. And, isn't it funny how everyone seems to think that *someone else* is the problem?

What are we to do? We can't seem to live with one another, but we can't live without one another.

Woody Allen summarized our predicament at the end of his movie, *Annie Hall*, when he turned to the camera and said:

> *I was complaining to my shrink the other day that my brother is driving me crazy — he thinks he's a chicken.*
>
> *My shrink said, "Well, then, just stay away from him. If it bothers you so much, just avoid him."*
>
> *"I'd like to," I replied, "but I need the eggs."*

That's our dilemma: How do we live in community with other people? How can we live and work together, getting the "eggs" we need without hurting each other. How do we accomplish this difficult goal . . . without having to walk on eggshells?

Those who deserve love the least need it the most.

~ from a North Carolina church marquee

The Fourfold Way

I've always loved Angeles Arrien's four basic principles for life:

1. Show up.

2. Pay attention.

3. Tell the truth.

4. Don't be attached to an outcome.

These principles seem to me to be simple, powerful guidelines for living in integrity, love, community, compassion . . . and surrender.

The Paradoxical Commandments

People are illogical, unreasonable, and self-centered.
> *Love them anyway.*

If you do good, people will accuse you of selfish ulterior motives.
> *Do good anyway.*

If you are successful, you will win false friends and true enemies.
> *Succeed anyway.*

The good you do today will be forgotten tomorrow.
> *Do good anyway.*

Honesty and frankness make you vulnerable.
> *Be honest and frank anyway.*

The biggest men and women with the biggest ideas can be shot down by the smallest men and women with the smallest minds.
> *Think big anyway.*

People favor underdogs but follow only top dogs.
Fight for a few underdogs anyway.

What you spend years building may be destroyed
overnight.
Build anyway.

People really need help but may attack you if you do
help them.
Help people anyway.

Give the world the best you have and you'll get kicked in
the teeth.
Give the world the best you have anyway.

~ Kent M. Keith

Faith-fully learning
ACCEPTANCE . . .

Acknowledging the whole person

Coming to terms with flaws and failings

Committing to unconditional love

Embracing our humanity

Praising others' positive qualities

Taking time to listen patiently

Agreeing to mutual respect

Never trying to change others

Caring concern in all situations

Expressing appreciation

Heaven and Hell

A holy man was having a conversation with the Lord one day and said, "Lord, I would like to know what Heaven and Hell are like."

The Lord led the holy man to two doors. He opened one of the doors, and the holy man looked in. In the middle of the room was a large round table.

In the middle of the table was a large pot of savory stew that smelled delicious. But the people sitting around the table were thin and sickly — they appeared to be famished. They were holding spoons with very long handles, but each found it impossible to reach into the pot of stew and take a spoonful, because the handle was longer than their arms and they could not get the spoons back into their mouths. The holy man shuddered at the sight.

The Lord said, "You have seen Hell."

They went to the next room, and he opened the door. It was exactly the same as the first one. There was the large round table with the large pot of savory stew. They were equipped with the same long-handled spoons, and were well-nourished, laughing, and talking.

The holy man said, "I don't understand."

"It is simple," said the Lord, "You see, here in Heaven, the people have learned to use their long spoons to reach across the table and feed each other."

The deepest need of man . . .

is the need to overcome his separateness,

to leave the prison of his aloneness.

~ Erich Fromm, therapist, author

Alone we can do so little;

together we can do so much.

~ Helen Keller, deaf and blind author and lecturer

Community

Psychiatrist Scott Peck, author of *The Road Less Traveled*, gave a lecture years ago in which he said that the biblical phrase, "The kingdom of God is within you," was mistranslated. If you go back to the original Aramaic, in which the Bible was first written, what that phrase really says is, "The kingdom of God is *among* you." The kingdom of God is in community. "Wherever two or more are gathered, God is there."

We are social creatures, meant to live in groups, clans, families, tribes, villages, neighborhoods, parishes — in partnership with others. When we come together and share who we are with one another, something magical happens. That's why support groups are so healing. It's why self-help programs are so successful — they tap into the power of community.

It took me many years to find connection and community in my own life. I often joke that "I'm a recovering Lone Ranger." It would be funnier if it weren't so true. Many years went by before I could muster the courage and take a chance on opening up: sharing my feelings, thoughts, and experiences with others. Over time, people began to validate the fact that I wasn't alone, I wasn't crazy, and there was nothing wrong with me.

Secrets can make us sick and holding our fears and anxieties inside can indeed make you feel like you're the only person with doubts, fears, anxieties, and problems. Too many of us of have spent years worrying, *You're okay — I'm not okay.* Isn't it time to give that up?

I've learned that people will forget what you said;
people will forget what you did;
but people will never forget how you made them feel.

~ Maya Angelou, author, poet, actress

And do not say, regarding anything,

"I am going to do that tomorrow," but only,

"If God will."

~ The Koran 18:24-25

Surrender makes you . . .

FAITHFULL

Living a Life of Gratitude

Barn's burnt down —

now

I can see the moon.

~ Mizuta Masahide,
17th-century Japanese samurai

Scheduled Gratitude

My friend Sam Beasley taught me how to get more of
what I love in life. He calls it *active appreciation*; here's how
he explained it to me:

Sam asked: "Do you like where you live?"

I answered: "I love where I live!"

"Good. Then here's what you do. Every morning
and every evening, for ten minutes or so, walk through
your home and notice the things that you really love. An
old quilt your mother made, a vase you inherited from
your great aunt, a piece of furniture you treasure, a room
you love to spend time in, a piece of art, or whatever
it is that you love. Touch these things, run your fingers
over them, and say out loud, 'I love this; I'd like more of
this.' This is an act of 'active appreciation' in which you
tell the Universe that you are deeply grateful for these
blessings. You show appreciation and you ask for more.
The Universe is a giant YES machine — it will always
send you more of what you pay attention to."

Sam summarized: "If you don't like what you're
getting in your life, change your prayer. How you live
your life is a form of prayer; what you pay attention to
is a form of prayer; what you express gratitude for is a
form of prayer. If you want your life to be different, your
prayer must be different."

He added: "Schedule this time on your calendar, just as you would any other appointment. Because if you don't schedule it, you'll start forgetting to do it. This is scheduled gratitude, active appreciation."

"Once you've done that," he said, "start practicing active appreciation in other ways. When you walk your dog, look for three things to be grateful for. When you're driving to a business meeting, look for three things to be grateful for. When you're out running errands, look for three things to be grateful for. You want to train yourself into the gratitude habit."

I've been following Sam's instructions for some time now and the results are wonderful. I feel like a very rich woman. I walk around happy almost all the time. I notice what's right in my home, in my business, and in my life. I give gratitude for my pets as I stroke their fur. I am grateful for my home-based business and count my blessings when I sit down to write every day. I give thanks and appreciation for my wonderful family, my loving friends, my car, my garden, my sweet cats, and adorable dog.

I give thanks for money in the bank, and I say a quick prayer of gratitude every time a check arrives. I kiss the checks and say, "Thanks, God." I write "thank you" on every check I write, and I'm grateful I have money to pay my bills.

Sam taught me that gratitude is more than attitude — it's action.

If the only prayer you say in your whole life is "thank you," that would suffice.

~ Meister Eckhart, German theologian and mystic

Gratitude unlocks the fullness of life. It turns what we have into enough, and more. It turns denial into acceptance, chaos to order, confusion to clarity. It can turn a meal into a feast, a house into a home, a stranger into a friend. Gratitude makes sense of our past, brings peace for today, and creates a vision for tomorrow.

~ Melody Beattie, therapist, author

Weather Report

"Any day I'm vertical
is a good day" . . .
            that's what I always say.
And I give thanks for my health.

If you ask me,
            "How are you?"

I'll answer, "GREAT!"
            because in saying so,
                        I make it so.
And I give thanks I can choose my attitude.

When Life gives me dark clouds and rain,
            I appreciate the moisture
            which brings a soft curl to my hair.

When Life gives me sunshine,
            I gratefully turn my face up
            to feel its warmth on my cheeks.

When Life brings fog,
        I hug my sweater around me
        and give thanks for the cool shroud of mystery
        that makes the familiar
        seem different and intriguing.

When Life brings snow,
        I dash outside
        to catch the first flakes on my tongue,
        relishing the icy miracle that is a snowflake.

Life's events and experiences
are like the weather —
        they come and go,
        no matter what my preference.

So, what the heck?!
        I might as well decide to enjoy them.

For indeed,
        there IS a time for every purpose
                under Heaven.

Each season brings its own unique blessings,
        and I give thanks.

The Glad Game

Chellie Campbell is a talented actress, a successful businesswoman, a sharp poker player, and a fabulous storyteller. She's also a friend, and I count her as one of my blessings.

In her wonderful book, *The Wealthy Spirit*, Chellie describes how, when she was a girl, her mother taught her to play "The Glad Game." On days when Chellie came home from school complaining about something — a bully on the playground, a harsh teacher, a skinned knee, or difficult homework — Chellie's mom would hug her, kiss away her tears, and then suggest, "Okay, enough complaining. Let's play 'The Glad Game.'"

"The Glad Game" is another name for a Gratitude List. "The Glad Game" helps you focus on what's *right* in your world today, instead of what's wrong. Chellie's mom was a very wise woman, teaching her that no matter what your troubles, there are still plenty of things to be grateful for: a sunny day, good food to eat, a loving family, a house to live in, a family pet to love, a handful of friends to enjoy, and much, much more.

Chellie would follow her mother's suggestion:

"I'm glad I have you as my mom.

"I'm glad the weekend is almost here.

"I'm glad I have some nice clothes to wear to school.

"I'm glad I don't have to share my room with my sister anymore.

"I'm glad I get to watch TV when I finish my homework.

"I'm glad we have pie for dessert."

Playing "The Glad Game" is a terrific way to change your attitude in a hurry. We all slip into self-pity once in a while — after all, we're only human. The important thing is to cut short the pity party and shift into gratitude. An attitude of gratitude gets us much further in life than complaining and self-pity.

Thanks, Chellie. I'm glad you're my friend.

Let us rise up and be thankful, for if we didn't learn a lot today, at least we learned a little; and if we didn't learn a little, at least we didn't get sick; and if we got sick, at least we didn't die; so, let us all be thankful.

~ The Buddha

Rampage of Appreciation

"Thank you" are two of the most powerful words in the English language, but they may very well be the most underutilized.

We are quick to complain, but slow to compliment. We don't hesitate to point out what's wrong, but completely neglect to point out what's right. We're eager to find fault, but reluctant to praise. We lament our woes, but overlook our blessings.

Esther and Jerry Hicks, in their book, *Ask and It Is Given*, write:

> *A desire to appreciate is a very good first step; and then as you find more things that you would like to feel appreciation for, it quickly gains momentum. And as you want to feel appreciation, you attract something to appreciate. And as you appreciate it, then you attract something else to appreciate, until, in time, you are experiencing a Rampage of Appreciation.*

Don't you just love that image? . . . *a Rampage of Appreciation!* If you want more to be grateful for, start by being more grateful.

When it comes to life, the critical thing is whether you take things for granted or take them with gratitude.

~ G.K. Chesterton,
English-born Gabonese novelist,
essayist, and poet

Can you see the holiness in those things you take for granted — a paved road or a washing machine? If you concentrate on finding what is good in every situation, you will discover that your life will suddenly be filled with gratitude, a feeling that nurtures the soul.

~ Harold S. Kushner, author

A Thankful Spirit

A thankful spirit is a healthy spirit. As the twists and
turns of life lead to feelings of being out of control,
sometimes our attitude is all that we do have control
over. The following reflection may help you develop
a thankful attitude. Sometimes life is all about how we
look at it!

I am thankful for . . .

- the mess to clean after a party because it means I
  have been surrounded by friends.

- the taxes I pay because it means that I am employed.

- a lawn that needs mowing, windows that need
  cleaning, and gutters that need fixing because it
  means I have a home.

- my shadow who watches me work because it means I
  am out in the sunshine.

- the spot I find at the far end of the parking lot
  because it means I am capable of walking.

- all the complaining I hear about our government
  because it means we have freedom of speech.

- my huge heating bill because it means I am warm.

- the lady behind me in church who sings off-key because it means that I can hear.

- the alarm that goes off early in the morning hours because it means that I am alive.

- the piles of laundry and ironing because it means my loved ones are nearby.

- weariness and aching muscles at the end of the day because it means I have been productive.

This reflection was written by Nancie J. Carmody and first appeared in the newsletter of First Presbyterian Church in Lyons, New York. It was reprinted in Family Circle *magazine in 1999.*

Feeling gratitude and not expressing it is like

wrapping a present and not giving it.

~ William Arthur Ward, pastor, author, and teacher

Conclusion

We humans often act like willful children resisting the assistance of a loving parent. "I can do it myself!" we insist. Our bold assertions of self-sufficiency and self-determination belie our puny size and inherent limitations. As my mother used to say, we often get "too big for our britches."

We long to be captains of our own destiny, Masters of the Universe — until we captain ourselves right smack into an iceberg, or master ourselves into a mess we can't get out of.

It is only then that we realize we were mistaken. We forgot that God is the Captain of Destiny and God is the real Master of the Universe. It is only then that we wise up and plead for God to take over. We remind ourselves that God is the Pilot and we are the co-pilot — not vice versa. And we promise never to forget this.

But forget, we do. We forget who's in charge and we try to nudge God out of the driver's seat — again and again.

That's why surrender isn't a one-time thing — it's an all-the-time thing. Surrender is a process as much as an event. Sometimes surrender is one day at a time; sometimes it's one moment at a time.

Surrender seems to come in layers, some shallow, some deep. Surrender can be a profound watershed event — or it can be a soft, subtle shift.

Perhaps because they arise from desperation and self-caused trouble, prayers of surrender are some of the sweetest ever heard. They reveal our deepest heart's desire — to be at one with Source — to feel aligned with Divine Order — to maintain conscious contact with God. Whatever words we use to describe our hearts' longing, words always fall short, for how can they really capture our yearning to be reunited with the Numinous, the Sacred, the Holy?

St. Augustine's surrender prayer summarized the universal human condition:

"Our heart is restless until it rests in You."

German theologian Reinhold Niebuhr's Serenity Prayer is a much-loved classic — humble and simple, it covers all the bases:

"God, grant me the serenity to accept the things I cannot change, the courage the change the things I can, and the wisdom to know the difference. Thy will, not mine, be done."

Some people use, *"Thy will be done,"* as a frequent, everyday prayer of surrender.

One of my personal favorites is:

God, I offer myself to Thee, to build with me and do with me as Thou wilt. Relieve me of the bondage of self, that I may better do Thy will. Take away my difficulties, that victory over them may bear witness to those I would help — of Thy power, Thy will, and Thy way of life — may I do Thy will always.

(Third Step Prayer, AA)

Buddhists recite beautiful prayers of surrender from their holy text, the *Dhammapada*:

I take the stance of complete effacement of the Self in deep submission, to realize the ultimate Truth.

(Pali text)

Empty this boat o' mendicant. When emptied it will move unimpeded. Lust and hatred are thereby more easily removed, paving the way to Nirvana.

(verse 389)

Likewise, the Muslim *Qur'an* provides exquisite prayers of surrender:

Lo! The religion before Allah is the surrender . . . if they surrender, then truly will they be rightly guided in prayer.

Surah 2[19, 20])

O, ye who believe, completely efface yourselves in self-surrender when worshipping your Lord, and do good, that happily you may prosper.

(Surah 23[77])

From these and many more powerful prayers from cultures around the world, it seems that the human need to surrender to the Divine is universal. We are blessed to live at a time in history when we have easy access to spiritual scriptures and practices from ancient times and ancient cultures, as well as contemporary wisdom. And as Matthew Fox suggests in his book, *One River, Many Wells*, perhaps all spiritual wisdom is the same in its fundamentals. If God is like an underground river, when groups of thirsty seekers dig their wells they tap into universal spiritual water.

In closing, I want to thank you for reading my stories and poems — they are the offerings of a wounded healer. For, as Belgian priest Henri Nouwen explains, it is only through our own wounds that we are able to help each other heal. That which is the most personal is also the most universal.

Closing Prayer

I wanted to write something very special to give you at the close of this book, so thought I'd try writing a prayer. I'm not an expert in writing prayers — and some of the beauties in preceding chapters are a tough act to follow. But nonetheless, I gave it my best shot. After many versions and many drafts, here's my prayer:

"Okay, God, I give up.

I surrender.

I'm coming over to the winning side."

I surrender . . . .

About the Author

 BJ Gallagher is an inspirational author and speaker. She writes business books that educate and empower, women's books that enlighten and entertain, and gift books that inspire and inform. Whether her audience is corporate executives, working women, or college students, her message is powerful, positive, and practical. She motivates and teaches with empathy, understanding, and more than a little humor.

BJ's international bestseller, *A Peacock in the Land of Penguins* (Berrett-Koehler), has sold more than 350,000 copies in 23 languages. Her other books include: *It's Never Too Late to Be What You Might Have Been* (Viva Editions) and *Why Don't I Do the Things I Know Are Good For Me?* (Berkley).

BJ is a regular *Huffington Post* contributor. She has been featured on *CBS Evening News* with Bob Schieffer, the *Today Show* with Matt Lauer, Fox News, PBS, CNN, and hundreds of radio programs.

BJ also conducts seminars and delivers keynotes at conferences and professional meetings across the country. Visit her at *www.bjgallagher.com*.

Hampton Roads Publishing Company
. . . for the evolving human spirit

Hampton Roads Publishing Company publishes books
on a variety of subjects, including spirituality, health, and
other related topics.

For a copy of our latest trade catalog,
call 978-465-0504 or visit our website at
www.hamptonroadspub.com